THE EFFECTIVE DIABETIC COOKBOOK FOR BEGINNERS 2024

Delicious and Healthy Recipes to Manage Diabetes Effortlessly

MARY M. VANISH

DISCLAIMER:

The recipes and nutritional information provided in this book, "The Effective Diabetic Cookbook for Beginners 2024," are intended for informational purposes only. They are not intended as medical advice or to replace the advice of a qualified healthcare professional.

While every effort has been made to ensure the accuracy of the information presented, Mary M. Vanish and the publisher make no warranties or guarantees regarding the results of following the recipes or dietary advice in this book. Individual results may vary depending upon various factors, including but not limited to, your personal health history and dietary choices.

Before making any changes to your diet or lifestyle, including starting a new diet plan presented in this book, it is recommended that you consult with your healthcare provider or a registered dietitian.

Mary M. Vanish and the publisher disclaim responsibility for any adverse effects, loss, or damage allegedly arising from the use or application of any information or suggestions presented in this book.

ABOUT THE AUTHOR

Mary M. Vanish has dedicated her career to promoting health and wellness through nutritious and delicious cooking. With a passion for creating recipes that are both flavorful and diabetic-friendly, Mary aims to empower individuals with the knowledge and skills to manage their health through balanced eating.

As a certified nutritionist and experienced cook, Mary understands the challenges faced by individuals managing diabetes and strives to provide practical solutions through her recipes. Her approach emphasizes fresh, whole ingredients and mindful eating habits, ensuring that each meal not only supports health but also delights the taste buds. Mary believes that everyone deserves to enjoy meals that are nourishing and satisfying, regardless of dietary restrictions. Through "The Effective Diabetic Cookbook for Beginners 2024," Mary hopes to inspire readers to embrace a healthier lifestyle while savoring every bite.

Table of Contents

INTRODUCTION

WELCOME TO YOUR DIABETIC JOURNEY

Congratulations on taking the first step towards a healthier and more balanced lifestyle! Managing diabetes can seem daunting, but with the right tools, knowledge, and delicious recipes, you can take control of your health and enjoy every meal. "The Effective Diabetic Cookbook for Beginners 2024" is designed to guide you through this journey, offering practical advice, nutritional insights, and mouth-watering recipes that will make healthy eating a delightful experience.

UNDERSTANDING DIABETES AND DIET

Diabetes is a chronic condition that affects how your body processes glucose, a type of sugar that is a primary source of energy. Proper management of diabetes involves maintaining a balanced diet, monitoring blood sugar levels, and staying active. A well-structured meal plan is crucial for keeping your blood sugar levels stable and preventing complications.

hat are carefully crafted to meet the nutritional needs of individuals with diabetes. Each recipe focuses on balanced portions of carbohydrates, proteins, and fats, with an emphasis on whole, unprocessed foods. Our goal is to help you create meals that are not only healthy but also delicious and satisfying.

HOW TO USE THIS COOKBOOK

This cookbook is divided into easy-to-navigate chapters, each focusing on different meals and occasions. From energizing breakfasts to hearty dinners, quick snacks to indulgent desserts, and even special occasion meals, you'll find a variety of recipes that suit your taste and lifestyle. Each recipe includes detailed nutritional information, making it easy for you to track your intake and manage your diet effectively.

Here's a quick guide to help you get the most out of this cookbook:

☐ **Chapter Overviews**: Each chapter begins with an introduction that explains the importance of the meal and provides tips on how to make the most of it.
☐ **Nutritional Information**: Every recipe includes detailed nutritional information, including carbohydrate counts, to help you manage your blood sugar levels.

Meal Planning Tips: Throughout the book, you'll find helpful tips on meal planning, portion control, and grocery shopping to make your cooking experience seamless and enjoyable.

 Special Diets: We've included variations and substitutions for those who have additional dietary needs or preferences, such as gluten-free or vegetarian options.

ESSENTIAL KITCHEN TOOLS FOR DIABETIC COOKING

Having the right tools in your kitchen can make cooking easier and more enjoyable. Here are some essential items that will help you prepare the recipes in this cookbook:

 Measuring Cups and Spoons: Accurate measurements are key to managing portion sizes and nutritional content.

 Food Scale: A food scale can help you weigh ingredients precisely, ensuring you stick to the recommended serving sizes.

 Sharp Knives and Cutting Board: Good quality knives and a sturdy cutting board will make chopping and slicing ingredients a breeze.

 Non-Stick Cookware: Non-stick pans reduce the need for added fats, making your meals healthier.

 Blender or Food Processor: These appliances are great for making smoothies, soups, and sauces with ease.

☐ **Slow Cooker or Instant Pot**: Perfect for preparing meals ahead of time and ensuring tender, flavorful dishes.

TIPS FOR MEAL PLANNING AND GROCERY SHOPPING

Effective meal planning and smart grocery shopping are essential components of managing diabetes. Here are some tips to help you get started:

☐ **Plan Your Meals**: Take some time each week to plan your meals. This will help you stay on track with your diet and avoid last-minute unhealthy choices.

☐ **Create a Shopping List**: Based on your meal plan, make a detailed shopping list. Stick to it to avoid impulse buys that might not fit your dietary needs.

☐ **Shop the Perimeter**: Focus on the outer aisles of the grocery store, where fresh produce, lean proteins, and dairy are typically located. Avoid processed foods found in the inner aisles.

☐ **Read Labels**: Learn to read nutrition labels to identify hidden sugars and unhealthy ingredients. Look for products with minimal added sugars and high fiber content.

☐ **Stay Hydrated**: Don't forget to include healthy drinks in your meal plan. Staying hydrated is essential for overall health and can help manage blood sugar levels.

I hope this cookbook will inspire you to explore new flavors, enjoy the process of cooking, and most importantly, manage your diabetes with confidence and joy. Remember, every small step you take towards a healthier lifestyle counts. Let's embark on this delicious and rewarding journey together!

CHAPTER 1

GETTING STARTED

1. LEMON HERB CHICKEN WITH QUINOA

SERVING SIZE
☐ **Servings**: 4

COOKING TIME
☐ **Prep Time**: 20 minutes
☐ **Cooking Time**: 25 minutes

NUTRITION INFORMATION (PER SERVING)
☐ **Calories**: 320
☐ **Protein**: 28g
☐ **Carbohydrates**: 30g
☐ **Fiber**: 5g
☐ **Sugars**: 1g
☐ **Fat**: 10g
☐ **Saturated Fat**: 2g
☐ **Cholesterol**: 75mg
☐ **Sodium**: 180mg

INGREDIENTS
☐ **Chicken**:
o 4 boneless, skinless chicken breasts

- 2 tablespoons olive oil
- 2 tablespoons fresh lemon juice
- 1 tablespoon fresh thyme, chopped
- 1 tablespoon fresh rosemary, chopped
- 2 garlic cloves, minced
- Salt and pepper to taste

☐ **Quinoa**:
- 1 cup quinoa, rinsed
- 2 cups low-sodium chicken broth or water
- 1 tablespoon olive oil
- 1/2 cup diced bell peppers
- 1/2 cup diced onions
- 1/2 cup chopped fresh parsley
- Zest of 1 lemon
- Salt and pepper to taste

DIRECTIONS

1. **Marinate the Chicken**:
- In a small bowl, mix together the olive oil, lemon juice, thyme, rosemary, garlic, salt, and pepper.
- Place the chicken breasts in a resealable plastic bag or a shallowdish. Pour the marinade over the chicken, ensuring it's evenly coated. Seal the bag or cover the dish, and refrigerate for at least 20 minutes or up to 2 hours.

2. **Cook the Quinoa**:
- In a medium saucepan, bring the chicken broth or water to a boil.

- Add the quinoa, reduce the heat to low, cover, and simmer for about 15 minutes, or until the quinoa is cooked and the liquid is absorbed.
- Fluff the quinoa with a fork and set aside.

3. **Prepare the Vegetables**:
- In a large skillet, heat 1 tablespoon of olive oil over medium heat.
- Add the diced bell peppers and onions. Sauté for 5-7 minutes, or until the vegetables are tender.
- Stir in the cooked quinoa, lemon zest, and chopped parsley. Season with salt and pepper to taste. Keep warm.

4. **Cook the Chicken**:
- Preheat a grill or a large skillet over medium-high heat.
- Remove the chicken from the marinade and discard the remaining marinade.
- Grill or cook the chicken breasts for about 6-8 minutes on each side, or until the chicken is cooked through and has reached an internal temperature of 165°F (74°C).

5. **Assemble the Dish**:
- Serve the Lemon Herb Chicken over a bed of the warm quinoa mixture.
- Garnish with additional fresh herbs and a wedge of lemon, if desired.

2. GRILLED SALMON WITH AVOCADO SALSA

SERVINGS
☐ **Serving Size**: 4

TIME
☐ **Prep Time**: 15 minutes
☐ **Cooking Time**: 10 minutes

NUTRITION INFORMATION (PER SERVING)

☐ **Calories**: 350
☐ **Protein**: 25g
☐ **Carbohydrates**: 12g
☐ **Dietary Fiber**: 7g
☐ **Sugars**: 1g
☐ **Total Fat**: 23g
☐ **Saturated Fat**: 3g
☐ **Cholesterol**: 55mg
☐ **Sodium**: 220mg

INGREDIENTS

For the Salmon:
☐ 4 salmon fillets (about 6 oz each)
☐ 2 tablespoons olive oil
☐ 1 teaspoon paprika
☐ 1 teaspoon garlic powder
☐ 1 teaspoon ground cumin
☐ Salt and pepper to taste
For the Avocado Salsa:
☐ 2 ripe avocados, diced
☐ 1 medium tomato, diced
☐ 1 small red onion, finely chopped

- 1 jalapeño, seeded and finely chopped (optional)
- 1/4 cup fresh cilantro, chopped
- Juice of 1 lime
- Salt and pepper to taste

DIRECTIONS

1. **Prepare the Salmon**:
- Preheat your grill to medium-high heat.
- In a small bowl, combine the olive oil, paprika, garlic powder, ground cumin, salt, and pepper.
- Brush the salmon fillets with the olive oil mixture, ensuring they are evenly coated.

2. **Grill the Salmon**:
- Place the salmon fillets on the preheated grill, skin-side down.
- Grill for about 4-5 minutes per side, or until the salmon is cooked through and flakes easily with a fork. The internal temperature should reach 145°F (63°C).
- Remove the salmon from the grill and let it rest for a few minutes.

3. **Prepare the Avocado Salsa**:
- While the salmon is grilling, prepare the avocado salsa.
- In a medium bowl, combine the diced avocados, tomato, red onion, jalapeño (if using), and cilantro.
- Squeeze the lime juice over the mixture and season with salt and pepper to taste.
- Gently toss the ingredients together until well combined.

4. **Serve**:
- Place the grilled salmon fillets on serving plates.

- Spoon the avocado salsa over the top of each fillet.
- Serve immediately and enjoy!

3. TURKEY AND SPINACH STUFFED BELL PEPPERS

SERVINGS: 4

Prep Time: 20 minutes
Cooking Time: 40 minutes

Nutrition Information (per serving):

- Calories: 250
- Protein: 25g
- Carbohydrates: 20g
- Dietary Fiber: 6g
- Sugars: 8g
- Fat: 8g
- Saturated Fat: 2g
- Sodium: 300mg

Ingredients

- 4 large bell peppers (any color)
- 1 lb ground turkey
- 1 cup fresh spinach, chopped
- 1 cup cooked quinoa
- 1 small onion, finely chopped
- 2 cloves garlic, minced

- 1 cup diced tomatoes (canned or fresh)
- 1 tsp olive oil
- 1 tsp dried oregano
- 1 tsp dried basil
- 1/2 tsp salt
- 1/4 tsp black pepper
- 1/2 cup shredded mozzarella cheese (optional)

Directions

1. **Prepare the Bell Peppers:**
o Preheat your oven to 375°F (190°C).
o Cut the tops off the bell peppers and remove the seeds and membranes.
o Arrange the peppers in a baking dish, cut side up.
2. **Cook the Filling:**
o In a large skillet, heat the olive oil over medium heat.
o Add the chopped onion and minced garlic. Sauté until the onion is translucent, about 3-4 minutes.
o Add the ground turkey to the skillet and cook until browned, breaking it up with a spoon as it cooks.
o Stir in the chopped spinach, cooked quinoa, diced tomatoes, dried oregano, dried basil, salt, and black pepper. Cook for an additional 5 minutes, allowing the flavors to meld.
3. **Stuff the Peppers:**
o Spoon the turkey and spinach mixture evenly into each of the prepared bell peppers.
o If desired, sprinkle shredded mozzarella cheese on top of each stuffed pepper.
4. **Bake the Peppers:**

o Cover the baking dish with aluminum foil and bake in the preheated oven for 30 minutes.

o Remove the foil and bake for an additional 10 minutes, or until the peppers are tender and the cheese is melted and golden brown (if using cheese).

5. **Serve:**

o Carefully remove the stuffed peppers from the oven and let them cool slightly before serving.

o Enjoy the stuffed peppers warm, accompanied by a side salad or steamed vegetables for a complete meal.

4. SHRIMP AND VEGETABLE STIR-FRY

Serving Size 26
□ Serves: 4

Prep Time
□ 15 minutes

Cooking Time
□ 10 minutes

Nutrition Information (per serving)

□ Calories: 210
□ Protein: 23g
□ Carbohydrates: 12g
□ Dietary Fiber: 4g
□ Sugars: 6g

☐ Fat: 7g
☐ Saturated Fat: 1g
☐ Cholesterol: 150mg
☐ Sodium: 600mg

Ingredients

☐ 1 lb (450g) large shrimp, peeled and deveined
☐ 2 tbsp olive oil
☐ 1 red bell pepper, thinly sliced
☐ 1 yellow bell pepper, thinly sliced
☐ 1 cup broccoli florets
☐ 1 cup snap peas
☐ 1 carrot, julienned
☐ 3 cloves garlic, minced
☐ 1-inch piece ginger, minced
☐ 3 tbsp low-sodium soy sauce
☐ 2 tbsp oyster sauce
☐ 1 tbsp rice vinegar
☐ 1 tsp sesame oil
☐ 1 tbsp sesame seeds (optional, for garnish)
☐ 2 green onions, sliced (optional, for garnish)

Directions

1. **Prepare the Ingredients**: Start by prepping all your ingredients. Thinly slice the bell peppers, julienne the carrot, and mince the garlic and ginger. Have all the vegetables ready to go as stir-frying is a quick process.
2. **Heat the Oil**: In a large wok or skillet, heat the olive oil over medium-high heat.

3. **Cook the Shrimp**: Add the shrimp to the wok and stir-fry for about 2-3 minutes, or until they turn pink and are just cooked through. Remove the shrimp from the wok and set aside.

4. **Stir-Fry the Vegetables**: In the same wok, add the garlic and ginger and stir-fry for about 30 seconds until fragrant. Add the bell peppers, broccoli, snap peas, and carrot. Stir-fry the vegetables for about 4-5 minutes, until they are tender-crisp.

5. **Combine Shrimp and Vegetables**: Return the cooked shrimp to the wok with the vegetables.

6. **Add the Sauce**: In a small bowl, mix the soy sauce, oyster sauce, rice vinegar, and sesame oil. Pour the sauce over the shrimp and vegetables and stir well to coat everything evenly. Cook for an additional 1-2 minutes until everything is heated through.

7. **Serve**: Remove from heat and transfer to a serving dish. Garnish with sesame seeds and sliced green onions if desired. Serve immediately.

5. BAKED COD WITH TOMATO AND BASIL

Serving Size
Servings: 4
Prep Time
☐ Prep Time: 15 minutes

Cooking Time
☐ Cooking Time: 20 minutes

Nutrition Information (per serving)

- Calories: 180
- Protein: 25g
- Carbohydrates: 5g
- Fiber: 1g
- Sugars: 3g
- Fat: 7g
- Saturated Fat: 1g
- Cholesterol: 65mg
- Sodium: 320mg

Ingredients

- 4 cod fillets (about 6 ounces each)
- 2 cups cherry tomatoes, halved
- 1/4 cup fresh basil, chopped
- 3 cloves garlic, minced
- 2 tablespoons olive oil
- 1 tablespoon lemon juice
- Salt and pepper to taste
- Lemon wedges for serving

Directions

1. **Preheat the Oven**: Preheat your oven to 400°F (200°C).
2. **Prepare the Baking Dish**: Lightly grease a baking dish with a small amount of olive oil or cooking spray.
3. **Season the Cod**: Place the cod fillets in the prepared baking dish. Drizzle 1 tablespoon of olive oil and the lemon juice over the fillets. Season with salt and pepper to taste.

4. **Add Tomatoes and Garlic**: Scatter the halved cherry tomatoes and minced garlic evenly around the cod fillets in the baking dish.

5. **Bake the Cod**: Bake in the preheated oven for about 15-20 minutes, or until the cod is opaque and flakes easily with a fork. The tomatoes should be soft and slightly blistered.

6. **Add Fresh Basil**: Remove the baking dish from the oven and sprinkle the chopped fresh basil over the cod and tomatoes.

7. **Serve**: Serve the baked cod hot, with a side of lemon wedges for added flavor. This dish pairs well with a simple green salad or steamed vegetables.

TIPS

☐ **Use Fresh Ingredients**: For the best flavor, use fresh tomatoes and basil. If fresh basil is not available, dried basil can be used as a substitute.

☐ **Check for Doneness**: The cooking time may vary slightly depending on the thickness of the cod fillets. Be sure to check the fish at the 15-minute mark to avoid overcooking.

6. QUINOA AND BLACK BEAN STUFFED SWEET POTATOES

Servings
☐ Serving Size: 4

Cooking Time
☐ Prep Time: 15 minutes

□ Cooking Time: 45 minutes

Nutrition Information (per serving)

□ Calories: 300
□ Protein: 10g
□ Carbohydrates: 50g
□ Fiber: 10g
□ Sugars: 9g
□ Fat: 7g

Ingredients
□ 4 medium sweet potatoes
□ 1 cup quinoa, rinsed
□ 1 can (15 oz) black beans, drained and rinsed
□ 1 cup corn kernels (fresh or frozen)
□ 1 red bell pepper, diced
□ 1 small red onion, diced
□ 1 clove garlic, minced
□ 1 teaspoon ground cumin
□ 1 teaspoon chili powder
□ 1 tablespoon olive oil
□ Salt and pepper to taste
□ Fresh cilantro, chopped (for garnish)
□ Lime wedges (for serving)

Directions

1. **Preheat the Oven**: Preheat your oven to 400°F (200°C). Line a baking sheet with parchment paper or aluminum foil.
2. **Bake the Sweet Potatoes**: Wash the sweet potatoes thoroughly and pierce them several times with a fork. Place

them on the prepared baking sheet and bake for 45 minutes, or until they are tender and can be easily pierced with a fork.

3. **Cook the Quinoa**: While the sweet potatoes are baking, cook the quinoa. In a medium saucepan, bring 2 cups of water to a boil. Add the rinsed quinoa, reduce the heat to low, cover, and simmer for 15 minutes, or until the quinoa is tender and the water is absorbed. Fluff with a fork and set aside.

4. **Prepare the Filling**: In a large skillet, heat the olive oil over medium heat. Add the diced red onion and red bell pepper, and sauté for 5 minutes until softened. Add the minced garlic, ground cumin, and chili powder, and cook for another minute until fragrant.

5. **Combine Ingredients**: Add the black beans and corn to the skillet, and cook for another 5 minutes, stirring occasionally. Add the cooked quinoa to the mixture, and stir to combine. Season with salt and pepper to taste.

6. **Stuff the Sweet Potatoes**: Once the sweet potatoes are done baking, let them cool slightly. Cut each sweet potato in half lengthwise and carefully scoop out a portion of the flesh to create a well for the filling. Spoon the quinoa and black bean mixture into each sweet potato half, packing it in tightly.

7. **Serve**: Garnish the stuffed sweet potatoes with fresh cilantro and serve with lime wedges on the side. Enjoy this nutritious and flavorful dish warm.

CHAPTER 2
BREAKFAST

1. ENERGIZING BREAKFAST BURRITOS

Serving Size
Makes 4 burritos
Prep Time
15 minutes
Cooking Time
15 minutes

Nutrition Information (per serving)
☐ Calories: 300
☐ Protein: 20g
☐ Carbohydrates: 25g
☐ Fiber: 7g
☐ Sugars: 3g
☐ Fat: 12g
☐ Saturated Fat: 4g
☐ Sodium: 400mg

Ingredients

- 4 whole wheat tortillas
- 6 large eggs
- 1/4 cup low-fat milk
- 1 tablespoon olive oil
- 1 small red bell pepper, diced
- 1 small green bell pepper, diced
- 1 small red onion, diced
- 1 cup spinach, chopped
- 1/2 cup black beans, drained and rinsed
- 1/2 cup reduced-fat shredded cheddar cheese
- 1 avocado, sliced
- Salt and pepper to taste
- Salsa (optional, for serving)

Directions

1. **Prepare the Vegetables**: Begin by washing and dicing the red bell pepper, green bell pepper, and red onion. Chop the spinach and set aside.
2. **Cook the Vegetables**: Heat the olive oil in a large skillet over medium heat. Add the diced red bell pepper, green bell pepper, and red onion. Sauté for 5-7 minutes, or until the vegetables are tender.
3. **Scramble the Eggs**: In a medium bowl, whisk together the eggs, low-fat milk, salt, and pepper. Pour the egg mixture into the skillet with the vegetables and cook, stirring frequently, until the eggs are fully cooked and scrambled.
4. **Add the Spinach and Black Beans**: Stir in the chopped spinach and black beans into the egg and vegetable mixture. Cook for an additional 2-3 minutes, until the spinach is wilted and the beans are heated through.

5. **Assemble the Burritos**: Warm the whole wheat tortillas in the microwave for about 20 seconds to make them more pliable. Place a quarter of the egg mixture onto each tortilla. Sprinkle with reduced-fat shredded cheddar cheese and top with avocado slices.

6. **Roll the Burritos**: Fold in the sides of each tortilla and roll it up tightly from the bottom to the top. Ensure that the filling is secure inside the burrito.

7. **Serve and Enjoy**: Serve the breakfast burritos immediately with salsa on the side, if desired. These burritos can also be wrapped in foil and stored in the refrigerator for up to 2 days or frozen for up to 1 month. Reheat in the microwave before serving.

Tips

☐ **Customization**: Feel free to customize these burritos with your favorite vegetables, such as mushrooms or tomatoes, or add a bit of spice with some chopped jalapeños.

☐ **Meal Prep**: These breakfast burritos are perfect for meal prep. Simply prepare and assemble them in advance, then wrap each one in foil and store in the fridge or freezer for a quick and easy breakfast on busy mornings.

2. BLUEBERRY ALMOND OVERNIGHT OATS

Serving Size
☐ Serves: 2

Prep Time
☐ Prep Time: 10 minutes
☐ Cooking Time: None (Refrigeration Time: 6-8 hours)

Nutrition Information (per serving)

☐ Calories: 250
☐ Carbohydrates: 38g
☐ Fiber: 8g
☐ Sugars: 8g
☐ Protein: 8g
☐ Fat: 10g

Ingredients

☐ 1 cup rolled oats
☐ 1 cup unsweetened almond milk
☐ 1/2 cup fresh or frozen blueberries
☐ 2 tablespoons chia seeds
☐ 2 tablespoons sliced almonds
☐ 1 tablespoon almond butter
☐ 1 teaspoon vanilla extract
☐ 1/2 teaspoon ground cinnamon
☐ Sweetener of choice (optional, such as stevia or monk fruit)

Directions

1. **Combine Ingredients**: In a medium-sized mixing bowl, combine the rolled oats, almond milk, chia seeds, almond

butter, vanilla extract, and ground cinnamon. Stir well to ensure all ingredients are evenly distributed.

2. **Add Blueberries and Almonds**: Gently fold in the blueberries and sliced almonds. If using frozen blueberries, there's no need to thaw them beforehand.

3. **Sweeten if Desired**: If you prefer a sweeter taste, add your choice of sweetener to the mixture and stir until fully incorporated.

4. **Refrigerate**: Divide the mixture into two jars or airtight containers. Seal and refrigerate for at least 6-8 hours, or overnight. This allows the oats to absorb the liquid and soften.

5. **Serve**: In the morning, give the oats a good stir. If the mixture is too thick for your liking, you can add a splash of additional almond milk to reach your desired consistency.

6. **Garnish and Enjoy**: Top with extra blueberries and almonds if desired, and enjoy your ready-to-eat Blueberry Almond Overnight Oats!

Tips

☐ **Make Ahead**: Prepare multiple servings in separate containers to have a healthy breakfast ready for several days.

☐ **Customization**: Feel free to swap blueberries with other berries or add additional toppings such as coconut flakes, flax seeds, or a dollop of Greek yogurt.

☐ **Portable**: These oats are perfect for on-the-go. Simply grab a jar from the fridge and take it with you for a convenient and nutritious breakfast.

3. SPINACH AND FETA SCRAMBLE

Serving Size
☐ Serves 2

Cooking time
☐ 10 minutes

Prep Time
☐ 5 minutes

Nutrition Information (per serving)

☐ Calories: 200
☐ Protein: 14g
☐ Carbohydrates: 4g
☐ Fiber: 1g
☐ Sugars: 2g
☐ Fat: 15g
☐ Saturated Fat: 7g
☐ Cholesterol: 270mg
☐ Sodium: 400mg

Ingredients

☐ 4 large eggs
☐ 1 cup fresh spinach, chopped
☐ 1/4 cup feta cheese, crumbled
☐ 1 tablespoon olive oil or butter
☐ Salt and pepper to taste

☐ 1/4 teaspoon garlic powder (optional)
☐ 1/4 teaspoon dried oregano (optional)

Directions

1. **Prepare the Ingredients**: Begin by chopping the fresh spinach and crumbling the feta cheese. Crack the eggs into a bowl and whisk them until the yolks and whites are fully combined. Season the eggs with a pinch of salt, pepper, and optional garlic powder and dried oregano for extra flavor.

2. **Heat the Pan**: Place a non-stick skillet or frying pan over medium heat. Add the olive oil or butter and let it melt and coat the pan evenly.

3. **Cook the Spinach**: Add the chopped spinach to the pan. Cook for 1-2 minutes, stirring frequently, until the spinach is wilted and tender.

4. **Add the Eggs**: Pour the beaten eggs into the pan with the spinach. Allow the eggs to sit undisturbed for about 30 seconds, then gently stir with a spatula. Continue to cook, stirring occasionally, until the eggs are mostly set but still slightly runny.

5. **Add the Feta**: Sprinkle the crumbled feta cheese over the eggs. Gently fold the eggs over the feta, allowing the cheese to melt slightly and the eggs to finish cooking. This should take an additional 1-2 minutes.

6. **Serve**: Once the eggs are fully cooked and the feta is warm, remove the pan from the heat. Serve the spinach and feta scramble immediately, garnished with an extra sprinkle of pepper if desired.

Tips for the Perfect Scramble

- **Low and Slow**: Cooking the eggs over medium heat ensures they stay tender and fluffy.
- **Fresh Ingredients**: Use fresh spinach and high-quality feta for the best flavor.
- **Customize**: Feel free to add other ingredients like diced tomatoes, bell peppers, or onions to the scramble for added texture and taste.

4. GREEK YOGURT PARFAIT WITH FRESH BERRIES

SERVING SIZE: 1 PARFAIT PREP TIME: 10 MINUTES COOKING TIME: NONE

Nutrition Information (per serving):

- Calories: 150
- Protein: 10g
- Carbohydrates: 20g
- Fiber: 3g
- Sugars: 15g
- Fat: 3g
- Saturated Fat: 1g
- Sodium: 60mg

☐ Calcium: 150mg

Ingredients:

☐ 1 cup plain Greek yogurt
☐ 1/2 cup fresh berries (strawberries, blueberries, raspberries, or a mix)
☐ 1 tablespoon honey or a sugar substitute (optional)
☐ 1/4 cup granola (preferably low-sugar)
☐ Fresh mint leaves for garnish (optional)

Directions:

1. **Prepare the Berries**: Wash the berries thoroughly under cold running water. Pat them dry with a clean kitchen towel or paper towels. If using strawberries, hull and slice them into smaller pieces.
2. **Sweeten the Yogurt**: If you prefer a sweeter parfait, mix the Greek yogurt with honey or a sugar substitute in a small bowl. Stir well until fully combined.
3. **Layer the Parfait**: Take a serving glass or a bowl and start by adding a layer of Greek yogurt at the bottom. Next, add a layer of fresh berries. Follow this with a layer of granola.
4. **Repeat the Layers**: Continue layering the yogurt, berries, and granola until you reach the top of the glass or bowl. Aim for two or three layers, depending on the size of your serving dish.
5. **Garnish and Serve**: Top the final layer with a few extra berries and a sprinkle of granola for a visually appealing finish. Garnish with fresh mint leaves if desired.

6. **Serve Immediately**: Greek Yogurt Parfait is best enjoyed immediately to keep the granola crunchy. If preparing ahead, keep the granola separate and add just before serving.

Tips for a Perfect Parfait:

☐ **Berry Selection**: Use a variety of berries to add different flavors and colors to your parfait. Fresh, in-season berries will offer the best taste and nutritional benefits.

☐ **Greek Yogurt**: Choose plain Greek yogurt to control the sugar content. You can also use flavored Greek yogurt but be mindful of the added sugars.

☐ **Granola**: Opt for a low-sugar granola to keep the parfait diabetic-friendly. Homemade granola can also be a great option if you want to control the ingredients.

5. AVOCADO AND SMOKED SALMON TOAST

Serving Size: 2 slices
Prep Time: 10 minutes Cooking Time: 5 minutes

Nutrition Information (per serving):

☐ Calories: 250 kcal
☐ Protein: 12g
☐ Carbohydrates: 20g
☐ Fiber: 6g

☐ Sugars: 2g
☐ Fat: 14g
☐ Saturated Fat: 3g
☐ Cholesterol: 15mg
☐ Sodium: 350mg

Ingredients:

☐ 2 slices whole grain bread (choose low-carb option for stricter diets)
☐ 1 ripe avocado
☐ 100g smoked salmon
☐ 1 tablespoon lemon juice
☐ Salt and pepper to taste
☐ Optional: fresh dill or chives for garnish

Directions:

1. **Toast the Bread**: Toast the slices of whole grain bread until golden brown and crisp.
2. **Prepare the Avocado**: While the bread is toasting, halve the avocado, remove the pit, and scoop the flesh into a small bowl. Mash the avocado with a fork until smooth. Add lemon juice, salt, and pepper to taste, mixing well.
3. **Assemble the Toast**: Spread the mashed avocado evenly over the toasted bread slices.
4. **Add Smoked Salmon**: Lay slices of smoked salmon on top of the avocado spread.
5. **Garnish (optional)**: Sprinkle with fresh dill or chives for added flavor and presentation.

6. **Serve**: Enjoy your Avocado and Smoked Salmon Toast immediately as a nutritious and satisfying breakfast or snack.

6. CHIA SEED PUDDING

Serving Size: 2 servings **Prep Time**: 5 minutes **Cooking Time**: 0 minutes

Ingredients:
- 1/4 cup chia seeds
- 1 cup unsweetened almond milk (or any milk of choice)
- 1-2 tablespoons maple syrup or honey (optional, adjust to taste)
- 1/2 teaspoon vanilla extract
- Fresh berries or sliced fruits for topping (optional)

Directions:

1. **Mix Ingredients**: In a mixing bowl or jar, combine chia seeds, almond milk, maple syrup (if using), and vanilla extract. Stir well to combine.
2. **Let it Sit**: Cover the bowl or jar and refrigerate for at least 4 hours, or preferably overnight. This allows the chia seeds to absorb the liquid and thicken into a pudding-like consistency.
3. **Stir Again**: After refrigerating for a while, give the mixture a good stir. This helps break up any clumps and ensures an even texture.
4. **Serve**: Divide the chia seed pudding into serving bowls or glasses. Top with fresh berries or sliced fruits if desired.

5. **Enjoy**: Chia seed pudding can be enjoyed immediately or kept refrigerated for up to 5 days. It makes a nutritious breakfast, snack, or dessert option, rich in fiber, omega-3 fatty acids, and protein.

Nutrition Info (per serving):

- Calories: 150
- Total Fat: 8g
  o Saturated Fat: 1g
  o Trans Fat: 0g
- Cholesterol: 0mg
- Sodium: 80mg
- Total Carbohydrate: 15g
  o Dietary Fiber: 10g
  o Sugars: 3g
- Protein: 5g

CHAPTER 3

LUNCH

1. GRILLED CHICKEN AND QUINOA SALAD

Prep Time: 15 minutes
Cooking Time: 20 minutes
Servings: 4

Ingredients:

- ☐ 1 cup quinoa
- ☐ 2 cups water or chicken broth
- ☐ 2 boneless, skinless chicken breasts
- ☐ 1 tablespoon olive oil
- ☐ Salt and pepper, to taste
- ☐ 1 red bell pepper, diced
- ☐ 1 cucumber, diced
- ☐ 1/4 cup red onion, finely chopped
- ☐ 1/4 cup fresh parsley, chopped
- ☐ 1/4 cup feta cheese, crumbled (optional)

For the Dressing:

- ☐ 1/4 cup olive oil
- ☐ 2 tablespoons lemon juice
- ☐ 1 clove garlic, minced
- ☐ 1 teaspoon Dijon mustard
- ☐ Salt and pepper, to taste

Directions:

1. **Cook Quinoa**: Rinse quinoa under cold water. In a medium saucepan, bring water or chicken broth to a boil. Add quinoa, reduce heat to low, cover, and simmer for 15 minutes or until quinoa is cooked and liquid is absorbed. Fluff with a fork and let cool.
2. **Prepare Chicken**: Preheat grill or grill pan over medium-high heat. Rub chicken breasts with olive oil and season with salt and pepper. Grill for about 6-7 minutes per side, or until internal temperature reaches 165°F (75°C) and juices run clear. Remove from heat and let rest for 5 minutes before slicing into strips.
3. **Make Dressing**: In a small bowl, whisk together olive oil, lemon juice, minced garlic, Dijon mustard, salt, and pepper until well combined.
4. **Assemble Salad**: In a large mixing bowl, combine cooked quinoa, grilled chicken strips, diced bell pepper, cucumber, red onion, and chopped parsley. Pour dressing over the salad and toss gently to coat.
5. **Serve**: Divide the salad into 4 servings. If desired, sprinkle each serving with crumbled feta cheese for added flavor.

Nutrition Information (per serving):

- Calories: 380 kcal
- Protein: 28g
- Carbohydrates: 30g
  - Dietary Fiber: 4g
  - Sugars: 2g
- Fat: 16g
  - Saturated Fat: 3g
- Cholesterol: 65mg
- Sodium: 280mg

Notes:
This Grilled Chicken and Quinoa Salad is not only delicious and satisfying but also packed with protein, fiber, and essential nutrients. It makes a perfect main dish for lunch or a light dinner, providing balanced nutrition while fitting into a diabetic-friendly diet. Adjust seasoning and ingredients according to your taste preferences and dietary needs.

2. TURKEY AND AVOCADO WRAP

Serving Size: 1 wrap **Prep Time:** 10 minutes **Cooking Time:** 0 minutes

Ingredients:

- 1 large whole wheat or low-carb tortilla
- 3 slices of deli turkey breast
- 1/4 avocado, sliced

- ☐ 1/4 cup shredded lettuce
- ☐ 2 slices of tomato
- ☐ 1 tablespoon hummus or Greek yogurt (optional)
- ☐ Salt and pepper to taste

Nutrition Information (per wrap):

- ☐ Calories: 250
- ☐ Carbohydrates: 26g
- ☐ Protein: 18g
- ☐ Fat: 10g
- ☐ Fiber: 7g
- ☐ Sugars: 2g

Directions:
1. Lay the tortilla flat on a clean surface. 2. If using, spread hummus or Greek yogurt evenly over the tortilla. 3. Layer the turkey slices, avocado slices, shredded lettuce, and tomato slices in the center of the tortilla. 4. Season with salt and pepper to taste. 5. Fold the sides of the tortilla over the filling, then roll tightly from the bottom to form a wrap. 6. Cut the wrap in half diagonally. 7. Serve immediately, or wrap tightly in foil or plastic wrap for later.
2. **Tip:** Customize your wrap by adding sliced cucumber, bell peppers, or a drizzle of balsamic glaze for extra flavor!

3. LENTIL AND VEGETABLE SOUP

Serving Size: 4 **Prep Time**: 15 minutes

Cooking Time: 30 minutes **Nutrition Information** (per serving):
- Calories: 250 kcal
- Total Fat: 3g
- Saturated Fat: 0.5g
- Cholesterol: 0mg
- Sodium: 600mg
- Total Carbohydrates: 45g
- Dietary Fiber: 12g
- Sugars: 8g
- Protein: 14g

Ingredients:
- 1 cup dried brown lentils, rinsed
- 4 cups vegetable broth (low-sodium)
- 1 onion, diced
- 2 carrots, diced
- 2 celery stalks, diced
- 2 garlic cloves, minced
- 1 teaspoon ground cumin
- 1 teaspoon dried thyme
- 1 bay leaf
- Salt and pepper, to taste
- 2 cups chopped spinach or kale
- Juice of 1 lemon

Directions:

1. In a large pot, combine lentils and vegetable broth. Bring to a boil over medium-high heat.
2. Reduce heat to medium-low and simmer for 15 minutes, uncovered.
3. Add diced onion, carrots, celery, minced garlic, ground cumin, dried thyme, bay leaf, salt, and pepper. Stir to combine.
4. Continue to simmer for another 15 minutes, or until lentils and vegetables are tender.
5. Stir in chopped spinach or kale and cook for an additional 2-3 minutes, until wilted.
6. Remove bay leaf and discard. Stir in fresh lemon juice for a refreshing flavor.
7. Taste and adjust seasoning if needed. Serve hot, optionally garnished with fresh herbs or a dollop of yogurt.

4. MEDITERRANEAN CHICKPEA SALAD

Serving Size: 4
Prep Time: 15 minutes
Cooking Time: 0 minutes (no cooking required)

Nutrition Information per Serving:
☐ Calories: 250 kcal
☐ Protein: 8g
☐ Carbohydrates: 30g
☐ Fiber: 8g

- Fat: 12g
- Saturated Fat: 2g
- Sodium: 350mg

Ingredients:
- 1 can (15 oz) chickpeas, drained and rinsed
- 1 cup cherry tomatoes, halved
- 1 cucumber, diced
- 1/2 red onion, thinly sliced
- 1/2 cup Kalamata olives, pitted and halved
- 1/4 cup fresh parsley, chopped
- 1/4 cup crumbled feta cheese (optional)
- 1/4 cup extra virgin olive oil
- 2 tablespoons red wine vinegar
- 1 clove garlic, minced
- 1 teaspoon dried oregano
- Salt and pepper to taste

Directions:
1. **Prepare the Dressing:**
o In a small bowl, whisk together olive oil, red wine vinegar, minced garlic, dried oregano, salt, and pepper. Set aside.
2. **Assemble the Salad:**
o In a large mixing bowl, combine chickpeas, cherry tomatoes, cucumber, red onion, Kalamata olives, and chopped parsley.
3. **Add the Dressing:**
o Pour the dressing over the salad ingredients in the bowl. Toss gently to coat everything evenly.
4. **Serve:**

o If using, sprinkle crumbled feta cheese over the top of the salad.

o Serve immediately, or refrigerate for 30 minutes to allow flavors to meld before serving.

Tips:

☐ This Mediterranean Chickpea Salad can be served as a light lunch or a refreshing side dish.

☐ Customize the salad by adding or substituting ingredients such as bell peppers, artichoke hearts, or diced avocado.

☐ Store any leftovers in an airtight container in the refrigerator for up to 2 days.

5. SHRIMP AND ASPARAGUS STIR-FRY

Serving Size: 4 servings **Prep Time**: 15 minutes **Cooking Time**: 10 minutes **Total Time**: 25 minutes

Nutrition Information (per serving):

☐ Calories: 180 kcal

☐ Carbohydrates: 8g

☐ Protein: 25g

☐ Fat: 5g

☐ Sodium: 450mg

☐ Fiber: 4g

☐ Sugar: 4g

Ingredients:
- [ ] 1 lb (450g) large shrimp, peeled and deveined
- [ ] 1 lb (450g) asparagus, trimmed and cut into 2-inch pieces
- [ ] 1 red bell pepper, thinly sliced
- [ ] 2 cloves garlic, minced
- [ ] 1-inch piece of ginger, grated
- [ ] 2 tbsp low-sodium soy sauce
- [ ] 1 tbsp oyster sauce
- [ ] 1 tbsp rice vinegar
- [ ] 1 tsp sesame oil
- [ ] 1 tbsp olive oil or vegetable oil
- [ ] Salt and pepper, to taste
- [ ] Sesame seeds and chopped green onions for garnish (optional)

Directions:

1. **Prepare Ingredients**: Begin by peeling and deveining the shrimp if not already prepared. Trim the asparagus and cut it into 2-inch pieces. Thinly slice the red bell pepper. Mince the garlic and grate the ginger.

2. **Stir-Fry Shrimp**: Heat olive oil or vegetable oil in a large skillet or wok over medium-high heat. Add minced garlic and grated ginger, stirring constantly for about 30 seconds until fragrant.

3. **Cook Shrimp**: Add shrimp to the skillet in a single layer. Cook for 2-3 minutes, flipping halfway through, until shrimp turns pink and opaque. Remove shrimp from skillet and set aside.

4. **Stir-Fry Vegetables**: In the same skillet, add a bit more oil if needed. Add asparagus and red bell pepper. Stir-fry for 3-4 minutes until vegetables are tender-crisp.

5. **Combine Sauce**: In a small bowl, mix together low-sodium soy sauce, oyster sauce, rice vinegar, and sesame oil.
6. **Combine Everything**: Return shrimp to the skillet with the vegetables. Pour the sauce over the mixture. Stir-fry for another 1-2 minutes, allowing the flavors to combine and the sauce to thicken slightly. Season with salt and pepper to taste.
7. **Serve**: Remove from heat and serve immediately, garnished with sesame seeds and chopped green onions if desired. Serve over brown rice or quinoa for a complete meal.

6. SPINACH AND CHICKEN STUFFED PEPPERS

Prep Time: 15 minutes **Cooking Time:** 30 minutes **Servings:** 4

Ingredients:
- 4 large bell peppers (any color)
- 1 tablespoon olive oil
- 1 small onion, finely chopped
- 2 cloves garlic, minced
- 1 cup cooked chicken breast, diced
- 2 cups fresh spinach, chopped
- 1 cup cooked quinoa (optional)
- 1 teaspoon dried oregano
- Salt and pepper, to taste
- 1/2 cup shredded mozzarella cheese (optional)

Directions:

1. **Preheat the Oven**: Preheat your oven to 375°F (190°C). Line a baking dish with parchment paper or lightly grease with olive oil.

2. **Prepare the Peppers**: Cut the tops off the bell peppers and remove the seeds and membranes. Place them upright in the prepared baking dish.

3. **Prepare the Filling**: In a large skillet, heat olive oil over medium heat. Add chopped onion and garlic, sautéing until softened and fragrant, about 3-4 minutes.

4. **Cook Chicken and Spinach**: Add diced chicken breast to the skillet and cook until heated through. Stir in chopped spinach and cook until wilted, about 2-3 minutes. If using, add cooked quinoa and mix well.

5. **Season and Fill Peppers**: Season the mixture with dried oregano, salt, and pepper to taste. Spoon the filling into the hollowed-out bell peppers until they are full and slightly overflowing. If desired, top each pepper with shredded mozzarella cheese.

6. **Bake**: Cover the baking dish with foil and bake in the preheated oven for 20 minutes. Remove the foil and bake for an additional 10 minutes, or until the peppers are tender and the cheese is melted and bubbly.

7. **Serve**: Remove from the oven and let cool slightly before serving. Garnish with fresh herbs like parsley or basil, if desired. Enjoy your nutritious and delicious Spinach and Chicken Stuffed Peppers!

Nutrition Information (per serving):

☐ Calories: 250 kcal
☐ Protein: 20g
☐ Carbohydrates: 20g

- Fiber: 4g
- Sugars: 6g
- Fat: 10g
- Saturated Fat: 3g
- Cholesterol: 45mg
- Sodium: 350mg

Note: Nutrition information may vary based on the specific ingredients and quantities used.

CHAPTER 4

DINNER

HERB-CRUSTED BAKED SALMON

Prep Time: 10 minutes **Cooking Time:** 15-20 minutes
Servings: 4

Ingredients:
- 4 salmon fillets (6 oz each), skin-on
- 2 tablespoons olive oil
- 2 tablespoons Dijon mustard
- 1/2 cup breadcrumbs (preferably whole wheat)
- 1/4 cup fresh parsley, chopped
- 1 tablespoon fresh dill, chopped
- 1 tablespoon fresh thyme leaves
- 2 cloves garlic, minced
- Salt and pepper to taste
- Lemon wedges, for serving

Directions:
1. **Preheat** your oven to 400°F (200°C). Line a baking sheet with parchment paper or lightly grease it.

2. **Prepare the Herb Crust:** In a small bowl, combine the breadcrumbs, chopped parsley, dill, thyme, minced garlic, salt, and pepper. Mix well.

3. **Prepare the Salmon:** Pat the salmon fillets dry with paper towels. Place them skin-side down on the prepared baking sheet.

4. **Coat the Salmon:** In another bowl, mix together the olive oil and Dijon mustard. Brush each salmon fillet evenly with the olive oil and mustard mixture.

5. **Apply the Herb Crust:** Press the herb breadcrumb mixture evenly onto the top of each salmon fillet, coating them completely.

6. **Bake the Salmon:** Transfer the baking sheet to the preheated oven and bake for 15-20 minutes, or until the salmon is cooked through and flakes easily with a fork.

7. **Serve:** Remove the salmon from the oven and let it rest for a few minutes. Serve hot, garnished with lemon wedges.

Nutrition Information (per serving):
- Calories: 350 kcal
- Protein: 34g
- Carbohydrates: 11g
- Fat: 18g
- Saturated Fat: 3g
- Cholesterol: 90mg
- Sodium: 350mg
- Fiber: 1g
- Sugar: 1g

Tips:
- Ensure your salmon fillets are of similar thickness for even cooking.

☐ Adjust the cooking time based on the thickness of your salmon fillets; thicker fillets may require a few extra minutes in the oven.

☐ Serve with steamed vegetables or a side salad for a complete meal.

BEEF AND BROCCOLI STIR-FRY

Serving Size: 4
Prep Time: 15 minutes
Cooking Time: 15 minutes

Nutrition Information per Serving:
☐ Calories: 280 kcal
☐ Carbohydrates: 12g
☐ Protein: 25g
☐ Fat: 15g
☐ Fiber: 4g
☐ Sodium: 600mg

Ingredients:
☐ 1 lb (450g) flank steak, thinly sliced against the grain
☐ 2 cups broccoli florets
☐ 1 red bell pepper, sliced
☐ 1 onion, sliced
☐ 3 cloves garlic, minced
☐ 1-inch piece of ginger, grated
☐ 1/2 cup low-sodium soy sauce

☐ 2 tbsp oyster sauce
☐ 1 tbsp cornstarch
☐ 1 tbsp sesame oil
☐ 2 tbsp vegetable oil
☐ Sesame seeds and green onions for garnish (optional)
☐ Cooked brown rice or cauliflower rice, for serving

Directions:

1. **Prepare the Sauce:**
o In a small bowl, whisk together soy sauce, oyster sauce, cornstarch, and grated ginger. Set aside.

2. **Marinate the Beef:**
o Place the thinly sliced flank steak in a bowl and pour half of the prepared sauce over it. Toss to coat evenly. Let it marinate for at least 10 minutes.

3. **Cook the Vegetables:**
o Heat 1 tbsp of vegetable oil in a large skillet or wok over medium-high heat. Add minced garlic and stir-fry for 30 seconds until fragrant.

o Add broccoli florets, sliced bell pepper, and onion to the skillet. Stir-fry for 3-4 minutes until vegetables are tender-crisp. Remove vegetables from the skillet and set aside.

4. **Cook the Beef:**
o In the same skillet, heat another tablespoon of vegetable oil over high heat. Add the marinated beef slices in a single layer. Let them sear without stirring for 1-2 minutes until browned.

o Stir-fry the beef for another 2-3 minutes until cooked through and slightly caramelized.

5. **Combine and Finish:**

o Return the cooked vegetables to the skillet with the beef. Pour the remaining sauce over the beef and vegetables.

o Stir everything together and cook for 1-2 minutes until the sauce has thickened and coats the beef and vegetables evenly.

6. **Serve:**

o Remove from heat and drizzle with sesame oil. Garnish with sesame seeds and chopped green onions if desired.

o Serve hot over cooked brown rice or cauliflower rice.

ZUCCHINI NOODLES WITH PESTO AND CHERRY TOMATOES

Serving Size: 2
Prep Time: 15 minutes
Cooking Time: 10 minutes

Nutrition Info (per serving):
☐ Calories: 250 kcal
☐ Carbohydrates: 10g
☐ Protein: 5g
☐ Fat: 22g
☐ Fiber: 4g
☐ Sugar: 5g
☐ Sodium: 300mg

Ingredients:
- 2 medium zucchinis
- 1 cup cherry tomatoes, halved
- 1/4 cup basil pesto (store-bought or homemade)
- 2 tablespoons olive oil
- Salt and pepper, to taste
- Grated Parmesan cheese (optional, for garnish)

Directions:

1. **Prepare the Zucchini Noodles:**
o Using a spiralizer or a vegetable peeler, create noodles from the zucchinis. If using a spiralizer, follow the manufacturer's instructions. If using a peeler, gently run it along the zucchini lengthwise to create long, thin strips resembling noodles.

2. **Cook the Cherry Tomatoes:**
o In a large skillet, heat 1 tablespoon of olive oil over medium heat. Add the halved cherry tomatoes and cook for 3-4 minutes, stirring occasionally, until they start to soften and release their juices.

3. **Cook the Zucchini Noodles:**
o In another skillet, heat the remaining olive oil over medium-high heat. Add the zucchini noodles and sauté for 2-3 minutes, tossing gently with tongs, until the noodles are just tender but still crisp.

4. **Combine the Ingredients:**
o Reduce the heat to low. Add the cooked cherry tomatoes to the skillet with the zucchini noodles. Stir in the basil pesto until everything is evenly coated. Cook for an additional 1-2 minutes, allowing the flavors to meld together. Season with salt and pepper to taste.

5. Serve:
o Divide the zucchini noodles with pesto and cherry tomatoes between two plates. Garnish with grated Parmesan cheese if desired. Serve warm and enjoy your delicious, low-carb meal!

GRILLED LEMON GARLIC CHICKEN

Prep Time: 10 minutes **Cooking Time:** 15 minutes
Servings: 4

Ingredients:
☐ 4 boneless, skinless chicken breasts
☐ 2 lemons, juiced and zested
☐ 4 cloves garlic, minced
☐ 2 tablespoons olive oil
☐ 1 teaspoon dried oregano
☐ Salt and pepper to taste
☐ Fresh parsley, chopped (for garnish, optional)

Directions:
1. **Marinate the Chicken:**
o In a bowl, combine lemon juice, lemon zest, minced garlic, olive oil, dried oregano, salt, and pepper. Mix well.

o Place the chicken breasts in a resealable plastic bag or shallow dish. Pour the marinade over the chicken, ensuring it is evenly coated. Marinate in the refrigerator for at least 30 minutes, or up to 4 hours for more flavor.

2. Preheat the Grill:

o Preheat your grill to medium-high heat. Clean and oil the grill grates to prevent sticking.

3. Grill the Chicken:

o Remove the chicken from the marinade, shaking off excess marinade. Discard the marinade.

o Grill the chicken breasts for about 6-7 minutes per side, or until they reach an internal temperature of 165°F (75°C). Cooking time may vary depending on the thickness of the chicken breasts.

4. Rest and Serve:

o Remove the chicken from the grill and let it rest for a few minutes before slicing or serving whole.

o Garnish with chopped fresh parsley, if desired, and serve with your favorite sides such as grilled vegetables, rice, or salad.

Nutrition Information (per serving):

- Calories: 250 kcal
- Total Fat: 10g
- Saturated Fat: 2g
- Cholesterol: 100mg
- Sodium: 300mg
- Total Carbohydrates: 4g
- Dietary Fiber: 1g
- Sugars: 1g
- Protein: 34g

SPAGHETTI SQUASH WITH TURKEY MARINARA

Serving Size: 4
Prep Time: 15 minutes
Cooking Time: 1 hour

Nutrition Information (per serving):
- Calories: 280
- Total Fat: 12g
- Saturated Fat: 2g
- Cholesterol: 60mg
- Sodium: 450mg
- Total Carbohydrate: 22g
- Dietary Fiber: 5g
- Sugars: 10g
- Protein: 20g

Ingredients:
- 1 medium spaghetti squash
- 1 lb lean ground turkey
- 1 onion, finely chopped
- 2 cloves garlic, minced
- 1 can (14 oz) crushed tomatoes
- 1 tablespoon tomato paste
- 1 teaspoon dried oregano
- 1 teaspoon dried basil
- Salt and pepper, to taste
- Fresh basil leaves, for garnish (optional)
- Grated Parmesan cheese, for serving (optional)

Directions:

1. **Prepare the Spaghetti Squash**:
o Preheat oven to 400°F (200°C).
o Cut the spaghetti squash in half lengthwise. Scoop out the seeds and pulp. Place the halves cut-side down on a baking sheet lined with parchment paper.
o Bake for 40-45 minutes, or until the squash is tender and easily pierced with a fork. Remove from oven and let cool slightly.

2. **Prepare the Turkey Marinara**:
o While the squash is baking, heat a large skillet over medium heat. Add the ground turkey and cook until browned, breaking it apart with a spoon as it cooks.
o Add the chopped onion and garlic to the skillet. Cook until the onion is translucent and the garlic is fragrant, about 3-4 minutes.
o Stir in the crushed tomatoes, tomato paste, dried oregano, dried basil, salt, and pepper. Bring to a simmer and let it cook for 10-15 minutes, stirring occasionally, until the flavors are well combined.

3. **Assemble and Serve**:
o Use a fork to scrape the flesh of the spaghetti squash into strands. Divide the squash among serving plates.
o Top each portion of spaghetti squash with a generous serving of turkey marinara sauce.
o Garnish with fresh basil leaves and grated Parmesan cheese, if desired.

4. **Enjoy**:
o Serve immediately and enjoy this delicious and nutritious meal!

VEGGIE-PACKED TURKEY MEATLOAF

Serving Size: 6 servings
Prep Time: 15 minutes
Cooking Time: 1 hour
Total Time: 1 hour 15 minutes

Ingredients:
- 1 lb ground turkey (preferably lean)
- 1 cup grated zucchini (excess water squeezed out)
- 1 cup grated carrots
- 1/2 cup finely chopped onion
- 2 garlic cloves, minced
- 1/2 cup rolled oats (or breadcrumbs)
- 1/4 cup ketchup (sugar-free)
- 1 tablespoon Worcestershire sauce (optional)
- 1 egg, beaten
- 1 teaspoon dried oregano
- 1 teaspoon dried basil
- Salt and pepper, to taste
- Olive oil spray or cooking spray

Directions:
1. **Preheat** your oven to 350°F (175°C). Lightly spray a loaf pan or baking dish with olive oil spray or coat with cooking spray.
2. **Prepare Vegetables:** Grate the zucchini and carrots, then squeeze out excess water from the zucchini using paper towels or a clean kitchen towel.

3. **Mix Ingredients:** In a large bowl, combine the ground turkey, grated zucchini, grated carrots, chopped onion, minced garlic, rolled oats (or breadcrumbs), ketchup, Worcestershire sauce (if using), beaten egg, dried oregano, dried basil, salt, and pepper. Mix until well combined.

4. **Form Loaf:** Transfer the turkey mixture into the prepared loaf pan or baking dish. Use your hands to shape it into a loaf shape, smoothing the top.

5. **Bake:** Place the meatloaf in the preheated oven and bake for about 1 hour, or until cooked through and the internal temperature reaches 165°F (75°C).

6. **Rest and Serve:** Remove the meatloaf from the oven and let it rest for 5-10 minutes before slicing. This allows the juices to redistribute.

7. **Serve:** Slice the meatloaf into thick slices and serve hot. You can pair it with steamed vegetables, mashed cauliflower, or a side salad for a complete meal.

Nutrition Information (per serving):
- Calories: 250 kcal
- Protein: 22g
- Carbohydrates: 15g
- Fiber: 3g
- Sugars: 5g
- Fat: 11g
- Saturated Fat: 3g
- Cholesterol: 90mg
- Sodium: 350mg

Note: This veggie-packed turkey meatloaf is a nutritious and flavorful twist on a classic comfort food. Packed with lean protein from turkey and nutrient-rich vegetables, it's a satisfying dish that fits well into a balanced diabetic meal plan. Enjoy the hearty flavors and the goodness of wholesome ingredients in every bite!

CHAPTER 5

SNACKS AND APPETIZERS

1. HUMMUS AND VEGGIE PLATTER

Serving Size:
□ Serves 4
Prep Time: 15 minutes
Cooking Time: None (Assembly only)

Nutrition Information (per serving):
□ Calories: 150
□ Total Fat: 8g
□ Saturated Fat: 1g
□ Cholesterol: 0mg
□ Sodium: 320mg
□ Total Carbohydrates: 16g
□ Dietary Fiber: 6g
□ Total Sugars: 2g
□ Protein: 6g

Ingredients:
☐ 1 cup of prepared hummus (store-bought or homemade)
☐ 1 cucumber, sliced
☐ 2 carrots, peeled and cut into sticks
☐ 1 bell pepper (red, yellow, or green), sliced
☐ 1 cup cherry tomatoes
☐ 1/2 cup Kalamata olives, pitted
☐ Fresh parsley or cilantro, for garnish (optional)
☐ Whole grain pita bread or crackers, for serving (optional)

Directions:
1. **Prepare the Vegetables:**
o Wash and cut the cucumber into slices.
o Peel and cut the carrots into sticks.
o Slice the bell pepper into strips.
o Arrange the vegetables on a large serving platter or tray.
2. **Assemble the Hummus:**
o Spoon the hummus into a serving bowl and place it in the center of the platter.
3. **Garnish and Serve:**
o Arrange the cherry tomatoes and Kalamata olives around the hummus bowl.
o Garnish with fresh parsley or cilantro if desired.
4. **Serve:**
o Serve immediately with whole grain pita bread or crackers on the side.

Tips:
☐ **Variations**: Feel free to add other vegetables such as celery, radishes, or broccoli florets.
☐ **Homemade Hummus**: To make your own hummus, blend chickpeas, tahini, garlic, lemon juice, olive oil, and salt until smooth.
☐ **Storage**: Store leftovers in an airtight container in the refrigerator for up to 2 days. However, hummus is best served fresh.

2. ROASTED CHICKPEAS

Ingredients:
☐ 1 can (15 oz) chickpeas (garbanzo beans), drained and rinsed
☐ 1 tablespoon olive oil
☐ 1/2 teaspoon salt (adjust to taste)
☐ 1/2 teaspoon paprika (optional, for added flavor)

Prep Time: 5 minutes
Cooking Time: 30 minutes
Servings: 4

Directions:
1. **Preheat your oven** to 400°F (200°C) and line a baking sheet with parchment paper or foil.
2. **Prepare the Chickpeas:**
o Drain and rinse the chickpeas thoroughly under cold water.

o Pat them dry with a paper towel to remove excess moisture. This step helps in achieving crispier roasted chickpeas.

3. Season the Chickpeas:
o In a bowl, toss the chickpeas with olive oil, salt, and paprika (if using). Ensure all chickpeas are evenly coated.
4. Roast in the Oven:
o Spread the seasoned chickpeas in a single layer on the prepared baking sheet.
o Roast in the preheated oven for about 30 minutes, or until chickpeas are crispy and golden brown. Shake the pan halfway through baking to ensure even cooking.
5. Cool and Serve:
o Once roasted, remove from the oven and let the chickpeas cool on the baking sheet for a few minutes.
o Serve warm as a snack or let them cool completely before storing in an airtight container for later use.

Nutrition Information (per serving):
☐ **Calories:** 120 kcal
☐ **Total Fat:** 4g
o **Saturated Fat:** 0.5g
o **Trans Fat:** 0g
☐ **Cholesterol:** 0mg
☐ **Sodium:** 300mg
☐ **Total Carbohydrate:** 16g
o **Dietary Fiber:** 4g
o **Sugars:** 0g
☐ **Protein:** 5g

3. GREEK YOGURT DIP WITH FRESH VEGGIES

Serving Size: 4 servings
Prep Time: 10 minutes
Cooking Time: 0 minutes

Nutrition Information (per serving):
- Calories: 80
- Total Fat: 4g
- Saturated Fat: 1g
- Cholesterol: 5mg
- Sodium: 120mg
- Total Carbohydrates: 6g
- Dietary Fiber: 1g
- Total Sugars: 4g
- Protein: 6g

Ingredients:
- 1 cup Greek yogurt (plain, non-fat)
- 1/2 cucumber, finely diced
- 1/2 red bell pepper, finely diced
- 1/2 yellow bell pepper, finely diced
- 1/4 cup cherry tomatoes, quartered
- 1 tablespoon fresh dill, chopped
- 1 tablespoon fresh parsley, chopped
- 1 clove garlic, minced
- 1 tablespoon lemon juice
- Salt and pepper to taste

Directions:

1. **Prepare the Vegetables**: Wash and finely dice the cucumber, red bell pepper, and yellow bell pepper. Quarter the cherry tomatoes.

2. **Mix the Dip**: In a mixing bowl, combine the Greek yogurt, diced vegetables (cucumber, red bell pepper, yellow bell pepper, cherry tomatoes), chopped dill, chopped parsley, minced garlic, and lemon juice. Mix well until all ingredients are evenly incorporated.

3. **Season**: Season the dip with salt and pepper to taste. Adjust seasoning according to your preference.

4. **Chill and Serve**: Cover the bowl with plastic wrap or transfer the dip to a serving dish. Refrigerate for at least 30 minutes to allow the flavors to meld together.

5. **Serve**: Serve chilled with a variety of fresh vegetables like carrot sticks, cucumber slices, celery sticks, and bell pepper strips. It also pairs well with whole grain crackers or pita chips.

4. ALMOND BUTTER ENERGY BALLS

Serving Size: Makes about 12 energy balls
Prep Time: 15 minutes
Cooking Time: No cooking required

Nutrition Information (per serving):
☐ Calories: 120 kcal
☐ Carbohydrates: 10g
☐ Protein: 4g
☐ Fat: 8g

- Fiber: 2g
- Sugar: 5g
- Sodium: 10mg

Ingredients:
- 1 cup rolled oats
- 1/2 cup almond butter
- 1/4 cup honey (or maple syrup for vegan option)
- 1/4 cup chopped almonds
- 2 tablespoons chia seeds
- 1/2 teaspoon vanilla extract
- Pinch of salt
- Optional: 1/4 cup mini chocolate chips or shredded coconut for coating

Directions:
1. **Mix Ingredients:** In a large bowl, combine rolled oats, almond butter, honey (or maple syrup), chopped almonds, chia seeds, vanilla extract, and a pinch of salt. Stir until well combined. If using, add mini chocolate chips or shredded coconut.
2. **Chill Mixture:** Place the mixture in the refrigerator for about 30 minutes to firm up. This will make it easier to roll into balls.
3. **Roll into Balls:** Once chilled, take about a tablespoon of the mixture and roll it into a ball using your hands. Repeat with the remaining mixture.
4. **Optional Coating:** If desired, roll the energy balls in shredded coconut or mini chocolate chips for added texture and flavor.
5. **Storage:** Store the almond butter energy balls in an airtight container in the refrigerator for up to two weeks.

Enjoy them as a quick snack or energy boost throughout the day!

5. BAKED ZUCCHINI CHIPS

Serving Size: 4 servings
Prep Time: 15 minutes
Cooking Time: 25 minutes

Nutrition Info per Serving:
- Calories: 90 kcal
- Carbohydrates: 10g
- Protein: 5g
- Fat: 4g
- Fiber: 3g
- Sugar: 3g
- Sodium: 200mg

Ingredients:
- 2 medium zucchinis, thinly sliced
- 1 tablespoon olive oil
- 1/4 cup grated Parmesan cheese (optional)
- 1/2 teaspoon garlic powder
- 1/2 teaspoon paprika
- Salt and pepper to taste

Directions:
1. **Preheat** your oven to 425°F (220°C). Line a baking sheet with parchment paper or lightly grease it.

2. **Slice** the zucchinis into thin rounds, about 1/8 inch thick. Pat them dry with a paper towel to remove excess moisture.
3. In a **medium bowl**, toss the zucchini slices with olive oil, garlic powder, paprika, salt, and pepper until evenly coated.
4. **Arrange** the zucchini slices in a single layer on the prepared baking sheet. Sprinkle grated Parmesan cheese over the slices, if using.
5. **Bake** in the preheated oven for about 20-25 minutes, or until the zucchini chips are golden brown and crispy. Flip the chips halfway through baking for even crispiness.
6. **Remove** from the oven and let cool slightly before serving. Enjoy your crispy Baked Zucchini Chips as a healthy snack or appetizer!

6. CAPRESE SKEWERS

Serving Size: Makes about 12 skewers
Prep Time: 15 minutes
Cooking Time: 0 minutes (No cooking required)

Nutrition Information (per skewer):
- Calories: 45 kcal
- Carbohydrates: 2 g
- Protein: 2 g
- Fat: 3 g
- Fiber: 1 g
- Sugar: 1 g
- Sodium: 60 mg

Ingredients:
- 24 cherry tomatoes
- 12 fresh small mozzarella balls (bocconcini)
- 24 fresh basil leaves
- Balsamic glaze (optional)
- Salt and pepper to taste
- 12 skewers (wooden or metal) **Directions:**

1. **Prepare Ingredients:**
- Rinse cherry tomatoes and basil leaves. Drain well.
- Drain mozzarella balls if in brine.

2. **Assemble Skewers:**
- On each skewer, thread one cherry tomato, followed by a basil leaf folded in half, then a mozzarella ball.
- Repeat with another cherry tomato, basil leaf, and mozzarella ball.
- Continue until skewer is filled, leaving space at each end for easy handling.

3. **Season and Serve:**
- Arrange prepared skewers on a serving platter.
- Drizzle with balsamic glaze (if using).
- Season lightly with salt and pepper to taste.

4. **Serve Immediately:**
- Caprese skewers are best served fresh.
- Enjoy as a delicious appetizer or light snack.

Tips:
- Choose ripe and firm cherry tomatoes for the best texture.
- If using wooden skewers, soak them in water for 30 minutes before assembling to prevent burning.
- Customize with additional ingredients like olives or a sprinkle of Italian seasoning for added flavor.

CHAPTER 6

DESSERTS

1. DARK CHOCOLATE AVOCADO MOUSSE

Serving Size: 4
Prep Time: 10 minutes
Cooking Time: 0 minutes

Nutrition Information (per serving):
- Calories: 180
- Total Fat: 12g
- o Saturated Fat: 3g
- o Trans Fat: 0g
- Cholesterol: 0mg
- Sodium: 5mg
- Total Carbohydrates: 19g
- o Dietary Fiber: 5g
- o Sugars: 10g
- Protein: 3g

Ingredients:
- ☐ 2 ripe avocados, peeled and pitted
- ☐ 1/4 cup unsweetened cocoa powder
- ☐ 1/4 cup maple syrup or honey (adjust to taste)
- ☐ 1/4 cup almond milk or any milk of your choice
- ☐ 1 teaspoon vanilla extract
- ☐ Optional toppings: fresh berries, shaved dark chocolate

Directions:
1. **Blend Avocados:** In a food processor or blender, combine the ripe avocados, unsweetened cocoa powder, maple syrup or honey, almond milk, and vanilla extract.
2. **Blend Until Smooth:** Blend until the mixture is smooth and creamy, scraping down the sides as needed to ensure everything is well combined.
3. **Chill (Optional):** For a firmer texture, refrigerate the mousse for 30 minutes to 1 hour before serving.
4. **Serve:** Divide the dark chocolate avocado mousse into serving dishes. Garnish with fresh berries and shaved dark chocolate if desired.
5. **Enjoy:** Serve chilled and enjoy this decadent dessert that's rich in healthy fats and antioxidants, perfect for satisfying your sweet cravings guilt-free.

2. BAKED APPLE WITH CINNAMON

Prep Time: 10 minutes
Cooking Time: 30 minutes
Servings: 2

Ingredients:
☐ 2 apples (use a variety that holds its shape well when baked, such as Granny Smith or Honeycrisp)
☐ 1 tablespoon unsalted butter, melted (or substitute with coconut oil for dairy-free option)
☐ 1 tablespoon brown sugar substitute (such as erythritol or stevia)
☐ 1/2 teaspoon ground cinnamon
☐ Pinch of nutmeg (optional)
☐ 1/4 cup chopped nuts (optional, for topping)

Directions:
1. **Preheat** your oven to 375°F (190°C).
2. **Prepare the Apples:**
o Wash the apples thoroughly and pat them dry.
o Using a sharp knife or an apple corer, carefully remove the core of each apple, leaving the bottom intact to create a well for the filling.
3. **Prepare the Filling:**
o In a small bowl, mix together the melted butter (or coconut oil), brown sugar substitute, cinnamon, and nutmeg (if using). Stir until well combined.
4. **Fill the Apples:**
o Place the cored apples in a baking dish or on a parchment-lined baking sheet.
o Spoon the cinnamon filling mixture evenly into each apple, filling the cavities where the cores were removed.
5. **Bake the Apples:**
o Bake in the preheated oven for about 30 minutes, or until the apples are tender and the filling is bubbling.
6. **Serve:**

o Remove from the oven and let cool slightly before serving.
o Optionally, sprinkle chopped nuts over the baked apples for added texture and flavor.

Nutrition Information (per serving):
- Calories: 150
- Total Fat: 5g
- Saturated Fat: 2g
- Cholesterol: 8mg
- Sodium: 1mg
- Total Carbohydrates: 28g
- Dietary Fiber: 5g
- Sugars: 18g
- Protein: 1g

Tips:
- Serve warm as is or with a dollop of Greek yogurt or a drizzle of sugar-free caramel sauce for a delightful dessert.
- Experiment with different apple varieties and adjust sweetness to your taste preferences by using more or less of the brown sugar substitute.

3. BERRY CHIA SEED PUDDING

Serving Size: 2
Prep Time: 10 minutes
Cooking Time: 0 minutes (plus chilling time)

Nutrition Info (per serving):
- Calories: 180 kcal

□ Carbohydrates: 20g
□ Protein: 5g
□ Fat: 10g
□ Fiber: 8g
□ Sugar: 8g
□ Sodium: 50mg

Chia seeds are packed with fiber, protein, and healthy fats, making them a perfect ingredient for a nutritious and delicious pudding. This Berry Chia Seed Pudding is not only easy to make but also a delightful treat for breakfast or dessert.

Ingredients:
□ 1/4 cup chia seeds
□ 1 cup unsweetened almond milk (or any milk of your choice)
□ 1/2 teaspoon vanilla extract
□ 1 tablespoon maple syrup (or sweetener of choice)
□ 1/2 cup mixed berries (fresh or frozen), plus extra for garnish
□ Optional toppings: sliced almonds, coconut flakes

Directions:
1. **Prepare the Base:** In a mixing bowl or jar, combine chia seeds, almond milk, vanilla extract, and maple syrup. Stir well to combine. Let it sit for 5 minutes and stir again to prevent clumping.
2. **Add Berries:** Gently mash half of the mixed berries with a fork or potato masher to release some juice. Add mashed and whole berries into the chia mixture. Stir gently to distribute the berries evenly.

3. **Chill:** Cover the bowl or jar and refrigerate for at least 2 hours, or preferably overnight. The chia seeds will absorb the liquid and thicken to a pudding-like consistency.

4. **Serve:** Before serving, give the pudding a good stir. Divide into serving bowls or jars. Top with extra berries and any optional toppings like sliced almonds or coconut flakes if desired.

5. **Enjoy:** Serve chilled and enjoy this creamy Berry Chia Seed Pudding as a nutritious breakfast, snack, or dessert!

4. ALMOND FLOUR CHOCOLATE CHIP COOKIES

Serving Size: Makes about 12 cookies
Prep Time: 15 minutes
Cooking Time: 12-15 minutes

Ingredients:
- 1 1/2 cups almond flour
- 1/4 cup coconut oil, melted
- 1/4 cup honey or maple syrup (adjust sweetness to taste)
- 1 teaspoon vanilla extract
- 1/4 teaspoon baking soda
- 1/4 teaspoon salt
- 1/2 cup dark chocolate chips (sugar-free if preferred)

Directions:

1. **Preheat** your oven to 350°F (175°C) and line a baking sheet with parchment paper.
2. **Mix** almond flour, melted coconut oil, honey or maple syrup, vanilla extract, baking soda, and salt in a bowl until well combined.
3. **Fold in** dark chocolate chips into the cookie dough mixture.
4. **Scoop** tablespoon-sized portions of dough and roll them into balls. Place them on the prepared baking sheet, spacing them about 2 inches apart.
5. **Flatten** each ball slightly with the palm of your hand or the back of a spoon.
6. **Bake** in the preheated oven for 12-15 minutes, or until the edges are golden brown.
7. **Cool** on the baking sheet for 5 minutes, then transfer to a wire rack to cool completely.

Nutrition Information (per cookie):

- Calories: 150
- Total Fat: 11g
  o Saturated Fat: 5g
  o Trans Fat: 0g
- Cholesterol: 0mg
- Sodium: 50mg
- Total Carbohydrate: 12g
  o Dietary Fiber: 2g
  o Sugars: 8g
- Protein: 3g

5. GREEK YOGURT AND BERRY POPSICLES

Prep Time: 10 minutes
Cooking Time: 0 minutes
Serving Size: Makes 6 popsicles

Nutrition Information (per popsicle):
☐ Calories: 80 kcal
☐ Carbohydrates: 10g
☐ Protein: 5g
☐ Fat: 2g
☐ Fiber: 2g
☐ Sugar: 7g
☐ Sodium: 20mg

Ingredients:
☐ 1 cup Greek yogurt (plain, unsweetened)
☐ 1 cup mixed berries (such as strawberries, blueberries, raspberries)
☐ 2 tablespoons honey or maple syrup (optional, adjust sweetness to taste)
☐ 1 teaspoon vanilla extract (optional)
☐ Popsicle molds
☐ Popsicle sticks

Directions:
1. **Prepare the Berries:**
o Wash the berries thoroughly and pat them dry with a paper towel. If using strawberries, hull and chop them into small pieces.
2. **Mix the Yogurt Base:**

o In a mixing bowl, combine the Greek yogurt, honey or maple syrup (if using), and vanilla extract (if using). Stir until smooth and well combined.

3. **Layer the Popsicles:**

o Spoon a small amount of the yogurt mixture into each popsicle mold, filling each mold about one-third full.

4. **Add the Berries:**

o Drop a few pieces of mixed berries into each mold, spreading them evenly.

5. **Fill with Yogurt:**

o Cover the berries with more of the yogurt mixture, filling each mold almost to the top.

6. **Insert Popsicle Sticks:**

o Place the popsicle sticks into each mold, ensuring they are centered. If your molds come with a lid that holds the sticks in place, use it to secure them.

7. **Freeze the Popsicles:**

o Place the popsicle molds in the freezer and freeze for at least 4-6 hours, or until completely solid.

8. **Serve:**

o Once frozen, remove the popsicles from the molds by running warm water over the outside of the molds for a few seconds. Gently pull on the sticks to release the popsicles.

o Enjoy these refreshing and nutritious Greek Yogurt and Berry Popsicles as a cool treat on a hot day!

6. COCONUT MACAROONS

Serving Size: Makes about 12 macaroons

Prep Time: 15 minutes
Cooking Time: 20 minutes **Ingredients:**
- ☐ 2 cups shredded unsweetened coconut
- ☐ 1/2 cup almond flour
- ☐ 1/2 cup sugar-free sweetener (erythritol or monk fruit)
- ☐ 2 large egg whites
- ☐ 1/4 teaspoon vanilla extract
- ☐ Pinch of salt

Directions:
1. **Preheat** your oven to 325°F (160°C). Line a baking sheet with parchment paper or a silicone baking mat.
2. **Mix** together the shredded coconut, almond flour, sugar-free sweetener, vanilla extract, and salt in a large bowl until well combined.
3. **Whisk** the egg whites in a separate bowl until they form stiff peaks.
4. **Fold** the whipped egg whites gently into the coconut mixture until everything is evenly incorporated.
5. **Scoop** about 2 tablespoons of the mixture onto the prepared baking sheet, forming each into a mound shape. Leave some space between each macaroon.
6. **Bake** in the preheated oven for 18-20 minutes, or until the macaroons are lightly golden on top.
7. **Cool** the macaroons on the baking sheet for a few minutes, then transfer them to a wire rack to cool completely.

Nutrition Information (per macaroon):
- ☐ Calories: 90 kcal
- ☐ Total Fat: 7g
- o Saturated Fat: 6g

- Total Carbohydrates: 4g
  - o Dietary Fiber: 2g
  - o Sugars: 1g
- Protein: 2g
- Sodium: 25mg

CHAPTER 7

DRINKS

GREEN SMOOTHIE

Serving Size:
1 smoothie
Prep Time:
5 minutes
Cooking Time:
0 minutes

Nutrition Information:
☐ Calories: Approximately 150 kcal
☐ Carbohydrates: 25g
☐ Protein: 5g
☐ Fat: 4g
☐ Fiber: 8g
☐ Sugar: 15g
☐ Sodium: 50mg

Ingredients:
- 1 cup fresh spinach leaves
- 1 ripe banana
- 1/2 cup frozen mango chunks
- 1/2 cup plain Greek yogurt
- 1 tablespoon chia seeds (optional)
- 1/2 cup almond milk (or any preferred milk)
- Honey or agave syrup (optional, for sweetness)
- Ice cubes (optional, for texture)

Directions:
1. **Prepare Ingredients**: Wash the spinach leaves thoroughly. Peel the banana and cut it into chunks if not using a high-speed blender. Measure out the frozen mango chunks, Greek yogurt, chia seeds (if using), and almond milk.
2. **Blend**: In a blender, add the spinach leaves, banana chunks, frozen mango chunks, Greek yogurt, chia seeds (if using), and almond milk. Optionally, add honey or agave syrup for sweetness and ice cubes for a thicker texture.
3. **Blend Until Smooth**: Start blending on low speed, gradually increasing to high, until the mixture is smooth and creamy. Pause and scrape down the sides of the blender with a spatula if needed to ensure all ingredients are well incorporated.
4. **Serve**: Pour the green smoothie into a glass. If desired, garnish with a sprinkle of chia seeds or a slice of banana on the rim. Serve immediately and enjoy the refreshing and nutritious green smoothie!

TIPS:

☐ For a thicker smoothie, add more frozen mango chunks or ice cubes.

☐ Adjust sweetness by adding more honey or agave syrup, or substitute with a sweeter fruit like pineapple.

☐ Customize with additional ingredients such as a scoop of protein powder, flaxseeds, or a handful of berries for added flavor and nutrients.

☐ ICED HERBAL TEA

Ingredients:
☐ 4 cups water
☐ 4 herbal tea bags (such as chamomile, peppermint, or hibiscus)
☐ Honey or stevia (optional, to taste)
☐ Fresh lemon slices or mint leaves for garnish (optional)
☐ Ice cubes

Directions:
1. **Boil Water**: In a kettle or saucepan, bring 4 cups of water to a boil.
2. **Steep Tea**: Remove the water from heat and add 4 herbal tea bags to the hot water. Cover and let steep for about 5-7 minutes, or until the tea is strong and flavorful.

3. **Sweeten (Optional)**: If desired, add honey or stevia to the hot tea and stir until dissolved. Adjust sweetness to your taste preference.

4. **Cool**: Allow the tea to cool to room temperature. You can speed up this process by placing the tea in the refrigerator for about 30 minutes.

5. **Serve Over Ice**: Fill tall glasses with ice cubes. Pour the cooled herbal tea over the ice.

6. **Garnish (Optional)**: Garnish each glass with a slice of lemon or a sprig of fresh mint for added freshness and flavor.

Serving Size:
This recipe makes approximately 4 servings.

- **Prep Time**: 5 minutes
- **Cooking Time**: 5-7 minutes (steeping time)

- **Nutrition Info** (per serving):
  o Calories: 0
  o Total Carbohydrates: 0g
  o Sugars: 0g
  o Sodium: 0mg
  o Protein: 0g

Tips:
- **Variations**: Experiment with different herbal tea blends such as chamomile, peppermint, hibiscus, or a blend of your favorite herbs.
- **Make Ahead**: Prepare a larger batch and store it in the refrigerator for a quick and refreshing drink throughout the day.

☐ **Health Benefits**: Herbal teas are known for their antioxidant properties and may offer various health benefits depending on the herbs used.

☐ CUCUMBER MINT INFUSED WATER

Serving Size:
☐ Makes approximately 8 cups (2 liters) of infused water.

Prep Time:
☐ 5 minutes
Cooking Time:
☐ 0 minutes (no cooking required)

Ingredients:
☐ 1 large cucumber, thinly sliced
☐ 10-12 fresh mint leaves
☐ Ice cubes (optional)
☐ Water (filtered or still water)

Directions:
1. **Prepare the Ingredients**: Wash the cucumber thoroughly and slice it thinly. Rinse the fresh mint leaves to remove any dirt or impurities.
2. **Combine Ingredients**: In a large pitcher or jar, add the sliced cucumber and fresh mint leaves.

3. **Add Water**: Fill the pitcher with water, covering the cucumber and mint completely. For best results, use filtered or still water.

4. **Infuse Flavors**: Refrigerate the infused water for at least 1-2 hours to allow the flavors of the cucumber and mint to infuse into the water. For a stronger flavor, you can refrigerate it overnight.

5. **Serve**: When ready to serve, you can add ice cubes to the pitcher for a refreshing chill. Pour into glasses, making sure each serving includes some cucumber slices and mint leaves for visual appeal.

Nutrition Information (per serving):
☐ Calories: 0
☐ Total Fat: 0g
☐ Sodium: 0mg
☐ Total Carbohydrates: 0g
☐ Dietary Fiber: 0g
☐ Sugars: 0g
☐ Protein: 0g

Tips:
☐ Experiment with the intensity of flavors by adjusting the amount of cucumber and mint.
☐ You can reuse the cucumber and mint for a second batch of infused water by adding more water to the pitcher once it's half-empty.
☐ Infused water can be stored in the refrigerator for up to 2 days. After that, the flavors may start to diminish.

☐ BERRY PROTEIN SHAKE

Serving Size: 1 serving
Prep Time: 5 minutes
Cooking Time: 0 minutes

Nutrition Info (per serving):
☐ Calories: 250 kcal
☐ Protein: 25g
☐ Carbohydrates: 30g
☐ Fat: 4g
☐ Fiber: 5g
☐ Sugar: 20g

Ingredients:
☐ 1 cup mixed berries (strawberries, blueberries, raspberries)
☐ 1 scoop vanilla protein powder
☐ 1 cup unsweetened almond milk (or any milk of your choice)
☐ 1 tablespoon chia seeds
☐ 1 tablespoon honey (optional, adjust sweetness to taste)
☐ Ice cubes (optional)

Directions:
1. **Prepare Ingredients**: Wash the berries thoroughly. If using fresh berries, remove stems or hulls as needed.
2. **Blend**: In a blender, combine the mixed berries, vanilla protein powder, unsweetened almond milk, chia seeds, and honey (if using). Add ice cubes if a colder shake is desired.

3. **Blend Until Smooth**: Blend on high speed until all ingredients are well combined and the shake reaches a smooth consistency.

4. **Serve**: Pour the berry protein shake into a glass. Optionally, garnish with a few fresh berries on top for presentation.

5. **Enjoy**: Sip and enjoy your delicious and nutritious Berry Protein Shake! This shake is perfect as a post-workout recovery drink or a satisfying breakfast option.

Tip: Feel free to customize your Berry Protein Shake by adding spinach or kale for extra greens, or substituting different fruits and flavors of protein powder to suit your taste preferences.

☐ LEMON GINGER DETOX DRINK

Ingredients
☐ 1 inch piece of fresh ginger, peeled and grated
☐ 1 lemon, juiced
☐ 4 cups of water
☐ Optional: Honey or stevia to taste

Directions
1. **Prepare the Ginger**: Peel and grate the fresh ginger using a fine grater.

2. **Boil Water**: In a saucepan, bring 4 cups of water to a boil.

3. **Infuse Ginger**: Add the grated ginger to the boiling water. Reduce heat and let it simmer for 5-10 minutes to infuse the water with ginger flavor.

4. **Add Lemon Juice**: Remove the saucepan from heat. Stir in the freshly squeezed lemon juice.

5. **Optional Sweetener**: If desired, add honey or stevia to taste for sweetness.

6. **Serve**: Pour the detox drink into mugs or glasses. You can strain out the ginger pulp if preferred.

Serving Size
This recipe makes approximately 4 servings.
- **Prep Time**: 5 minutes
- **Cooking Time**: 10 minutes (simmering time)
- **Total Time**: 15 minutes

Nutrition Information (per serving)
- Calories: 10
- Total Fat: 0g
- Sodium: 10mg
- Total Carbohydrates: 3g
- Dietary Fiber: 1g
- Sugars: 1g
- Protein: 0g

Benefits
- **Hydration**: Helps keep you hydrated, especially beneficial after waking up or during hot weather.
- **Digestive Aid**: Ginger supports healthy digestion and can help reduce nausea.
- **Detoxification**: Lemon provides vitamin C and antioxidants, aiding in detoxifying the body.

☐ **Antioxidants**: Both ginger and lemon are rich in antioxidants, which help combat oxidative stress in the body.

CHAPTER 8

SPECIAL OCCASIONS

☐ HOLIDAY ROASTED TURKEY BREAST

Serving Size: 4-6 servings
Prep Time: 15 minutes
Cooking Time: 1 hour 30 minutes

Ingredients:
☐ 1 turkey breast (about 2-3 pounds)
☐ 2 tablespoons olive oil
☐ 2 cloves garlic, minced
☐ 1 teaspoon dried rosemary
☐ 1 teaspoon dried thyme
☐ Salt and pepper, to taste

Directions:
1. **Preheat** your oven to 350°F (175°C).
2. **Prepare** the turkey breast by patting it dry with paper towels. Place it on a roasting rack in a roasting pan.
3. **Season** the turkey breast with salt and pepper, rubbing it evenly over the surface.

4. **In a small bowl**, mix together the olive oil, minced garlic, rosemary, and thyme.

5. **Rub** the olive oil mixture all over the turkey breast, ensuring it's evenly coated.

6. **Roast** the turkey breast in the preheated oven for about 1 hour 30 minutes, or until the internal temperature reaches 165°F (75°C) when measured with a meat thermometer inserted into the thickest part of the breast.

7. **Once done**, remove the turkey breast from the oven and let it rest for 10-15 minutes before slicing.

8. **Slice** the turkey breast and serve warm with your favorite side dishes, such as roasted vegetables or a fresh salad.

Nutrition Information (per serving):
- Calories: 250 kcal
- Protein: 30g
- Fat: 12g
- Carbohydrates: 0g
- Fiber: 0g
- Sugar: 0g
- Sodium: 300mg

☐ DIABETIC-FRIENDLY BBQ RIBS

Ingredients:
- 2 lbs pork ribs
- 1 cup sugar-free BBQ sauce
- 1 tsp paprika

- ☐ 1 tsp garlic powder
- ☐ Salt and pepper, to taste

Prep Time: 10 minutes
Cooking Time: 2 hours
 Servings: 4

Nutrition Information per Serving:
- ☐ Calories: 350
- ☐ Total Fat: 20g
- ☐ Saturated Fat: 7g
- ☐ **Cholesterol:** 90mg
- ☐ Sodium: 480mg
- ☐ Total Carbohydrates: 9g
- ☐ Fiber: 1g
- ☐ Sugars: 2g
- ☐ Protein: 30g

Directions:
1. **Preheat** your oven to 300°F (150°C).
2. **Prepare** the ribs by removing the membrane from the back of the rack, if not already done. Pat dry with paper towels.
3. **Season** the ribs with paprika, garlic powder, salt, and pepper, rubbing the seasoning evenly on both sides.
4. **Place** the ribs on a baking sheet lined with aluminum foil, meaty side up.
5. **Bake** in the preheated oven for 1.5 to 2 hours, or until the meat is tender and starts to pull away from the bones.
6. **Brush** the ribs with sugar-free BBQ sauce during the last 15 minutes of cooking, allowing the sauce to caramelize slightly.

7. **Remove** from the oven and let the ribs rest for a few minutes before serving.
8. **Serve** hot, accompanied by a side of coleslaw or grilled vegetables for a complete meal.

These diabetic-friendly BBQ ribs are not only delicious but also easy to prepare, making them perfect for family gatherings or special dinners. Enjoy the bold flavors and tender texture without compromising your health goals.

☐ BIRTHDAY CARROT CAKE

Serving Size: 8 slices
Prep Time: 20 minutes
Cooking Time: 40 minutes

Nutrition Information (per serving):
☐ Calories: 280
☐ Total Fat: 22g
o Saturated Fat: 10g
o Trans Fat: 0g
☐ Cholesterol: 65mg
☐ Sodium: 180mg
☐ Total Carbohydrates: 18g
o Dietary Fiber: 3g
o Sugars: 10g
☐ Protein: 6g

Ingredients:
☐ 2 cups almond flour

- ☐ 1 teaspoon baking powder
- ☐ 1/2 teaspoon baking soda
- ☐ 1/2 teaspoon salt
- ☐ 1 teaspoon ground cinnamon
- ☐ 1/2 teaspoon ground nutmeg
- ☐ 3 large eggs
- ☐ 1/2 cup coconut oil, melted
- ☐ 1/2 cup honey or sugar-free sweetener equivalent
- ☐ 1 teaspoon vanilla extract
- ☐ 2 cups grated carrots (about 3-4 medium carrots)
- ☐ 1/2 cup chopped nuts (optional)
- ☐ 1/4 cup unsweetened shredded coconut (optional)

Directions:
1. **Preheat** your oven to 350°F (175°C). Grease and flour a 9-inch round cake pan or line it with parchment paper.
2. In a large bowl, **whisk together** almond flour, baking powder, baking soda, salt, cinnamon, and nutmeg.
3. In another bowl, **beat** eggs, melted coconut oil, honey or sweetener, and vanilla extract until well combined.
4. **Gradually add** the wet ingredients to the dry ingredients, stirring until smooth. Fold in grated carrots, chopped nuts (if using), and shredded coconut (if using).
5. **Pour** the batter into the prepared cake pan, spreading it evenly.
6. **Bake** in the preheated oven for 35-40 minutes, or until a toothpick inserted into the center comes out clean.
7. **Remove** from the oven and allow the cake to cool in the pan for 10 minutes before transferring it to a wire rack to cool completely.

8. **Frost** with sugar-free cream cheese frosting or enjoy it as is. Optionally, garnish with additional shredded coconut or chopped nuts.

9. **Slice** and serve. Enjoy this moist and flavorful Birthday Carrot Cake as a delicious treat for any special occasion!

☐ VALENTINE'S DAY CHOCOLATE-COVERED STRAWBERRIES

Prep Time: 15 minutes
 Cooking Time: 10 minutes (chilling time)
Servings: 4

Ingredients:
☐ 1 pint fresh strawberries, washed and dried
☐ 4 ounces sugar-free dark chocolate, chopped
☐ Optional: Chopped nuts (e.g., almonds, pecans) or shredded coconut for coating

Directions:
1. **Prepare the Strawberries:**
o Wash the strawberries thoroughly under cold water and pat them dry with paper towels. Ensure they are completely dry to help the chocolate adhere well.
2. **Melt the Chocolate:**

o Place the chopped sugar-free dark chocolate in a microwave-safe bowl. Microwave in 30-second intervals, stirring each time until melted and smooth. Be careful not to overheat.

3. **Dip the Strawberries:**

o Line a baking sheet with parchment paper. Holding each strawberry by the stem, dip it into the melted chocolate, swirling to coat evenly. Allow any excess chocolate to drip back into the bowl.

4. **Optional Coating:**

o If desired, roll the chocolate-covered strawberries in chopped nuts or shredded coconut while the chocolate is still wet. This adds texture and extra flavor.

5. **Chill:**

o Place the dipped strawberries on the prepared baking sheet. Chill in the refrigerator for about 10 minutes or until the chocolate sets.

6. **Serve:**

o Arrange the chocolate-covered strawberries on a serving plate. Optionally, garnish with a dusting of powdered sugar or a drizzle of melted chocolate for an elegant presentation.

Nutrition Information (per serving):
☐ Calories: Approximately 120 kcal
☐ Carbohydrates: 15g
☐ Fat: 6g
☐ Protein: 2g
☐ Fiber: 4g
☐ Sugar: 8g
☐ Sodium: 5mg

☐ THANKSGIVING STUFFED ACORN SQUASH

Serving Size: 4
Prep Time: 20 minutes
Cooking Time: 45 minutes

Nutrition Info (per serving):
- Calories: 320
- Total Fat: 12g
- Saturated Fat: 2g
- Cholesterol: 0mg
- Sodium: 260mg
- Total Carbohydrates: 52g
- Dietary Fiber: 8g
- Sugars: 12g
- Protein: 6g

Ingredients:
- 2 acorn squash, halved and seeded
- 1 cup quinoa, rinsed
- 2 cups vegetable broth
- 2 cups fresh spinach, chopped
- 1/2 cup dried cranberries
- 1/2 cup pecans, chopped
- Optional: 1/4 cup crumbled feta cheese
- Salt and pepper, to taste
- Olive oil, for drizzling

Directions:
1. **Preheat the Oven**: Preheat your oven to 400°F (200°C).
2. **Prepare the Acorn Squash**: Place the acorn squash halves, cut side up, on a baking sheet. Drizzle with olive oil and sprinkle with salt and pepper. Roast in the preheated oven for about 30-35 minutes, or until squash is tender when pierced with a fork.
3. **Cook the Quinoa**: While the squash is roasting, prepare the quinoa. In a medium saucepan, bring the vegetable broth to a boil. Add the quinoa, reduce heat to low, cover, and

simmer for 15 minutes, or until quinoa is cooked and liquid is absorbed.

4. **Prepare the Filling**: In a large bowl, combine cooked quinoa, chopped spinach, dried cranberries, chopped pecans, and optional crumbled feta cheese. Season with salt and pepper to taste. Mix well to combine.

5. **Stuff the Squash**: Once the acorn squash halves are tender, remove from the oven. Fill each squash half with the quinoa mixture, pressing down gently to pack it in.

6. **Bake Again**: Return the stuffed squash to the oven and bake for an additional 10-15 minutes, or until heated through and lightly browned on top.

7. **Serve**: Remove from the oven and let cool slightly before serving. Garnish with additional chopped pecans or fresh herbs if desired. Enjoy your delicious Thanksgiving Stuffed Acorn Squash!

☐ NEW YEAR'S EVE SHRIMP COCKTAIL

Serving Size: 4 servings
Prep Time: 15 minutes
Cooking Time: 5 minutes

Nutrition Info (per serving):
☐ Calories: 120 kcal
☐ Protein: 24 g
☐ Carbohydrates: 4 g
☐ Fat: 1 g
☐ Fiber: 1 g

☐ Sugar: 1 g
☐ Sodium: 320 mg

Ingredients:
☐ 1 pound large shrimp, peeled and deveined
☐ 1 cup sugar-free cocktail sauce
☐ 1 lemon, cut into wedges
☐ Fresh herbs (parsley or dill) for garnish

Directions:
1. **Prepare the Shrimp:**
o Bring a pot of water to a boil. Add the shrimp and cook for 2-3 minutes, or until they turn pink and opaque. Avoid overcooking as shrimp can become rubbery.
o Drain the shrimp and transfer them to a bowl of ice water to cool quickly. Once cooled, drain again and pat dry with paper towels.
2. **Chill the Shrimp:**
o Refrigerate the cooked shrimp until ready to serve. Chilling helps to firm up the texture and enhances the flavor.
3. **Serve:**
o Arrange the chilled shrimp on a serving platter or individual cocktail glasses.
o Place a small bowl of sugar-free cocktail sauce in the center for dipping.
4. **Garnish:**
o Garnish with lemon wedges and fresh herbs like parsley or dill for added freshness and presentation.
5. **Enjoy:**

o Serve immediately as a delightful appetizer or main course for your New Year's Eve celebration. Pair with sparkling water or a light white wine for a festive touch.

CONCLUSION

Congratulations on completing your journey through "The Effective Diabetic Cookbook for Beginners 2024"! We hope this cookbook has inspired you to embrace a delicious and nutritious approach to managing diabetes.

Throughout this book, we've explored a variety of recipes designed to be both satisfying and supportive of your health goals. From energizing breakfasts to hearty dinners, quick snacks to indulgent desserts, each recipe was crafted with care to help you enjoy meals that are not only tasty but also promote stable blood sugar levels.

Remember, managing diabetes is about more than just what you eat—it's about making informed choices, staying active, and nurturing a positive relationship with food. By incorporating the principles and recipes from this cookbook into your daily routine, you're taking proactive steps towards a healthier lifestyle.

As you continue on your journey, we encourage you to explore new flavors, adapt recipes to suit your preferences, and above all, listen to your body's needs. Whether you're cooking for yourself, your family, or friends, may each meal be a celebration of health and well-being.

Thank you for allowing "The Effective Diabetic Cookbook for Beginners 2024" to be a part of your kitchen. Here's to many more delicious moments and a lifetime of good health!

APPENDIX

ADDITIONAL RESOURCES AND TIPS

1. GLOSSARY OF TERMS

☐ **Carbohydrates**: Includes sugars, starches, and fiber found in fruits, vegetables, grains, and dairy products.
☐ **Blood Glucose**: The sugar in your blood that provides energy to your body's cells.
☐ **Insulin**: A hormone that helps regulate blood sugar levels.
☐ **Glycemic Index (GI)**: A measure of how quickly foods raise blood glucose levels.
☐ **Portion Control**: Managing serving sizes to regulate calorie and nutrient intake.
☐ **Whole Grains**: Grains that contain the entire grain kernel, including bran, germ, and endosperm.

2. TIPS FOR DINING OUT

□ **Plan Ahead**: Check the restaurant's menu online beforehand to choose healthier options.
□ **Ask Questions**: Inquire about preparation methods and ingredient substitutions.
□ **Request Modifications**: Ask for sauces and dressings on the side or for grilled instead of fried options.
□ **Share Dishes**: Split large portions with a dining companion to manage portion sizes.

3. SUBSTITUTION GUIDE

□ **Sweeteners**: Replace sugar with alternatives like stevia, erythritol, or monk fruit sweetener.
□ **Flours**: Use almond flour, coconut flour, or flaxseed meal instead of traditional wheat flour.
□ **Fats**: Opt for healthy fats like olive oil, avocado oil, or nut butters instead of butter or lard.

4. MEASUREMENT CONVERSIONS

□ **Cups to Grams/Ounces**: Handy conversion table for commonly used ingredients.
□ **Oven Temperature Conversion**: Fahrenheit to Celsius conversions for baking.

5. UNDERSTANDING NUTRITION LABELS

☐ **Serving Size**: Pay attention to portion sizes and adjust nutritional values accordingly.

☐ **Total Carbohydrates**: Includes sugars, fiber, and other carbohydrates.

☐ **Sodium Content**: Monitor sodium intake for heart health and blood pressure management.

Printed in Great Britain
by Amazon

44435911R00066